I0419271

YESTERDAY, TODAY, & TOMORROW
volume 1, 2nd edition

slow fashioned in my own style
spring 2015 collection
by Larissa Louise Dahroug

UNLESS OTHERWISE NOTED

content by Larissa Louise Dahroug

garments by Larissa Louise Dahroug

photos by Larissa Louise & Omar Gawdat Dahroug

photographed onsite at Elk Cove Inn & Spa in Elk, California on the Mendocino Coast, Mother's Day weekend, 2015

photographed using standard cell phone cameras

photos edited using Google applications

first edition of this title available through blurb.com

this edition published using createspace.com

Fashions come and go. Style is timeless, so why not take my time?
-Larissa Louise, spring 2015

Dear Reader,

In response to cultural desire for instant gratification, lack of respect and knowledge of crafts-personship, process, technique and artistry, I invite you to Do It Yourself...or hire a professional to help create your personal style. Custom ensembles created with second hand, antique, vintage, retro, and repurposed materials may be a slow process, but I think you will find the results timeless.

Special thanks to my husband, Omar *(top right having a cup of coffee on the beach)* for planning our travel, helping me take photos, and continuing to support my creative efforts. Special thanks to my mother, Karen Louise Funyak *(bottom right smiling with one of my paintings, photo by my father, Joseph M. Funyak)* who taught me the value of making my own clothes and what it means to be beautiful.

Thanks to God for everything.

Always,
Larissa Louise

GLOSSARY OF TERMS

ANTIQUE -items 100 years of age or older.

CUSTOMIZE - to adapt something pre-frabricated to personal specifications.

DIY - short for: Do It Yourself. A philosophy.

FASHION - a popular style of dress from a specific time period

PATTERN - the set of instructions to make a specific item of clothing.

REPURPOSE - to use an item for something other than it's original intended use.

RETRO - a new item designed in the style of a past fashion.

SECOND HAND - a used item less than 20 years old.

SLOW FASHION - term coined by designer Kate Fletcher describing a social movement promoting sustainable apparel design, manufacture, and consumption practices over mass production and disposable trends.

STYLE - the unique or otherwise identifying way an individual or group of individuals wears garments.

UP-CYCLE - to modify and repurpose an item that is unusable in it's original form into something new and of value.

VINTAGE - items over 20 years old but less than 100 years old.

These are the patterns I customized in some of the garments featured in this DIY style collection.

Feathered friends don't belong in cages.
It is the same with women, Art, and style.
Set them free!

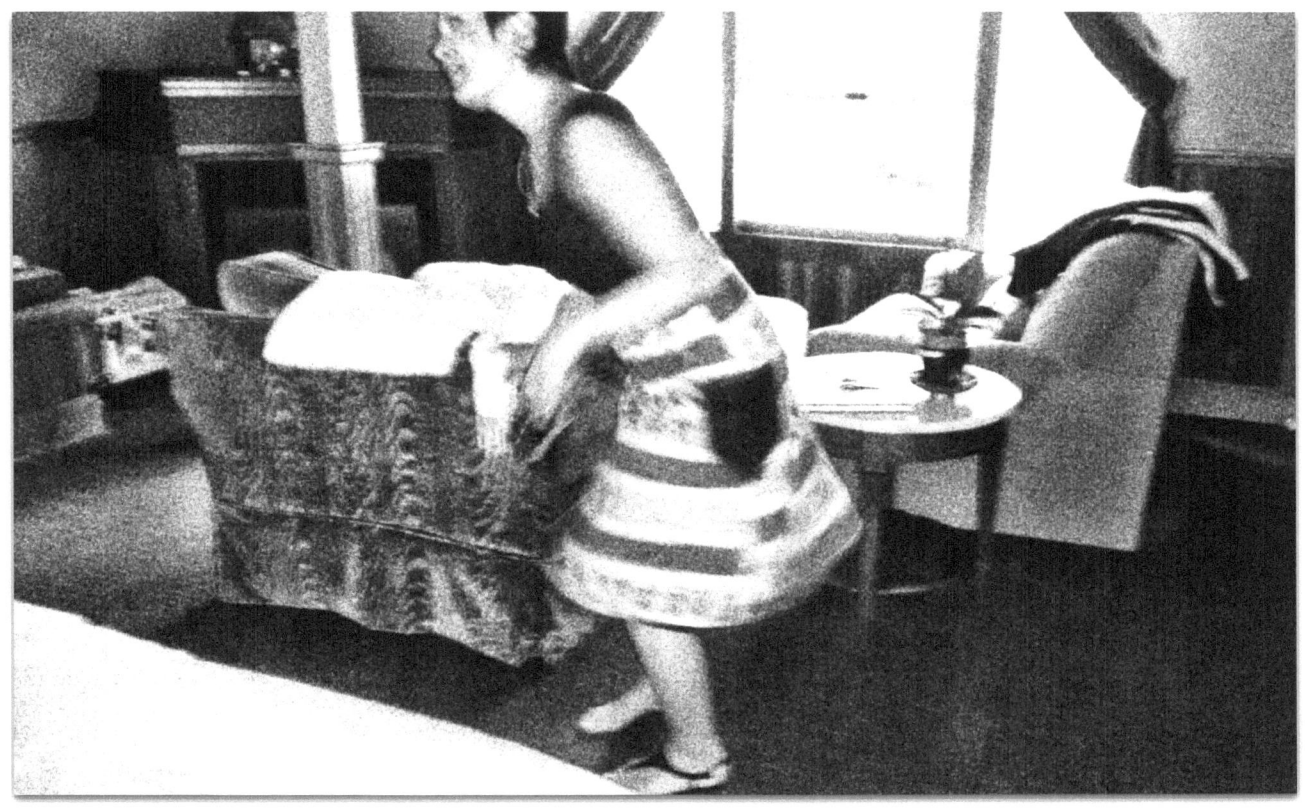

Check Mate Dress
one of a kind garment
customized from burda pattern 7798
dress materials: vintage (1970's) cotton blend chess print, denim purchased at scrap
depot, antique button purchased at a rummage sale, cotton quilt binding, thread
ensemble: vintage (1980's) gold tone leather braided belt, jelly sandals, my
grandmother's pearls

Fully Charged
self portrait

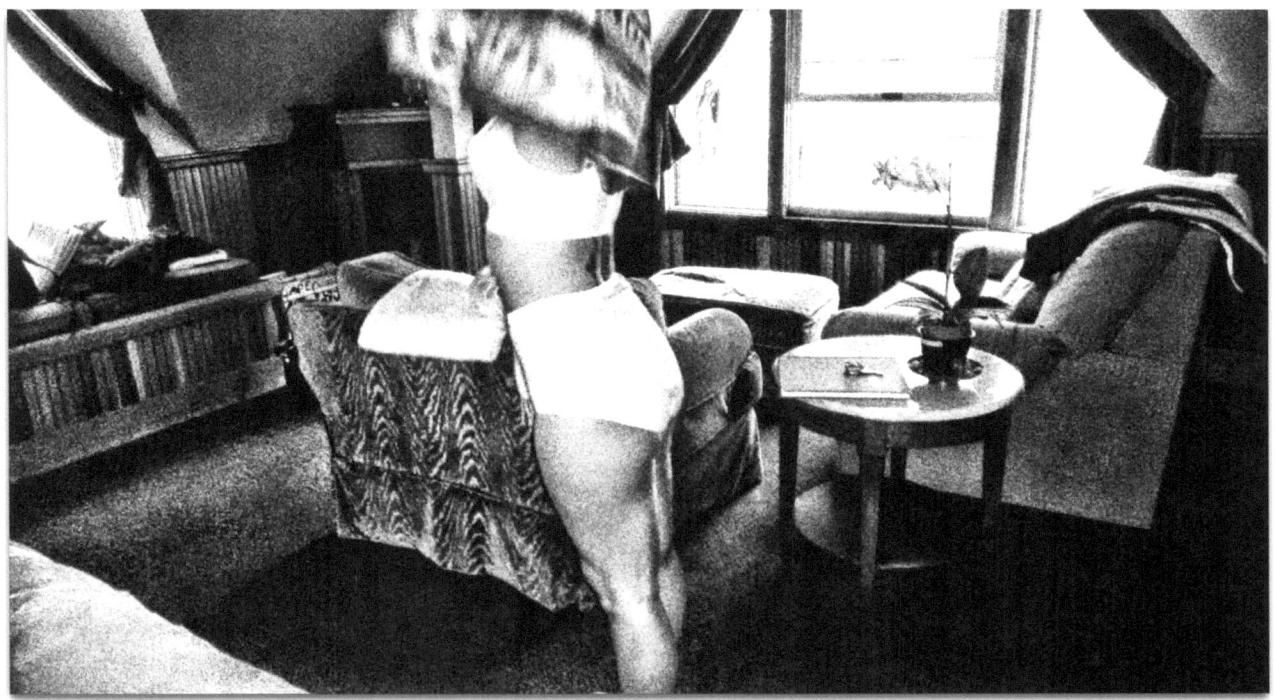

Under the Check Mate Dress…

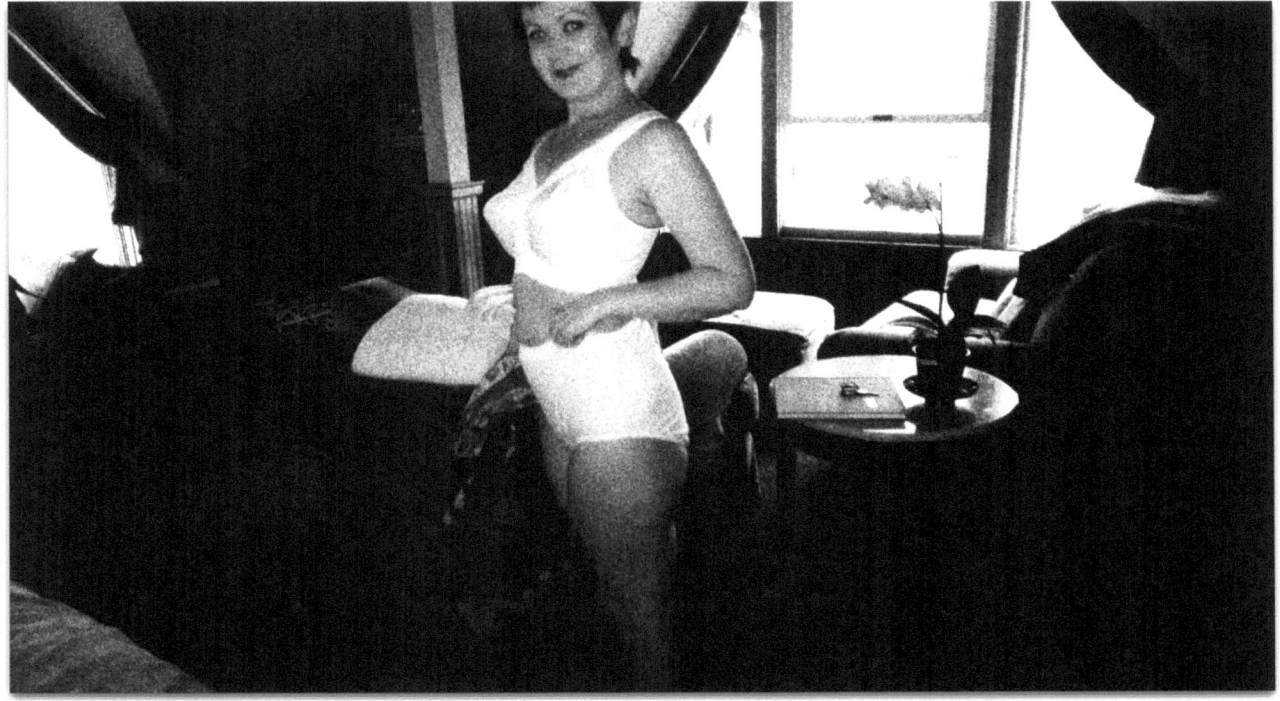

I Will Be Brief…for Hours
Platex 18 Hour Bra, Hanes cotton briefs

Some things are better purchased new.

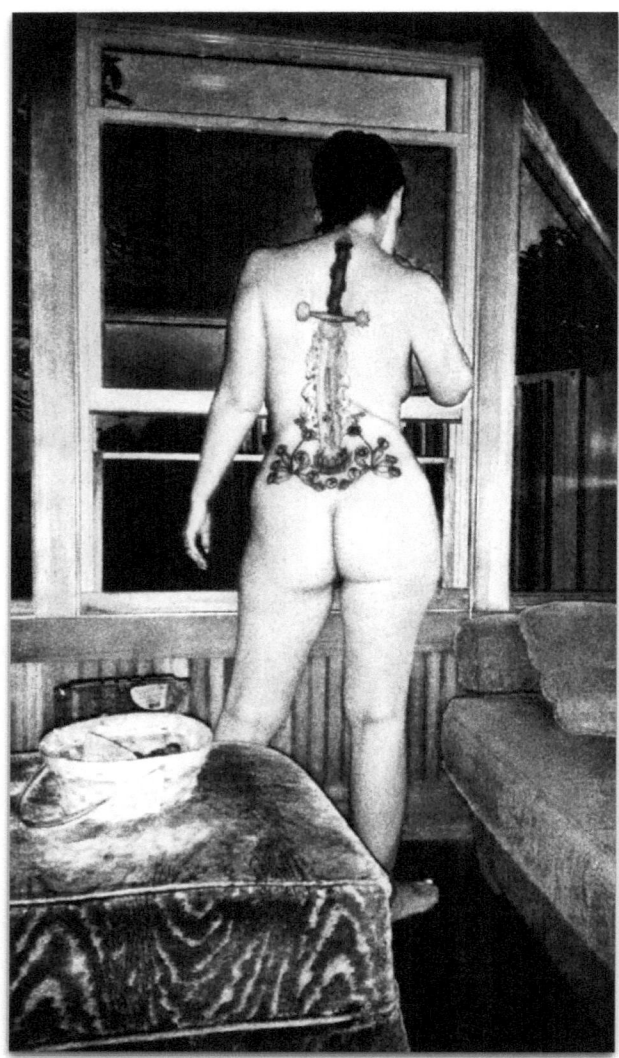

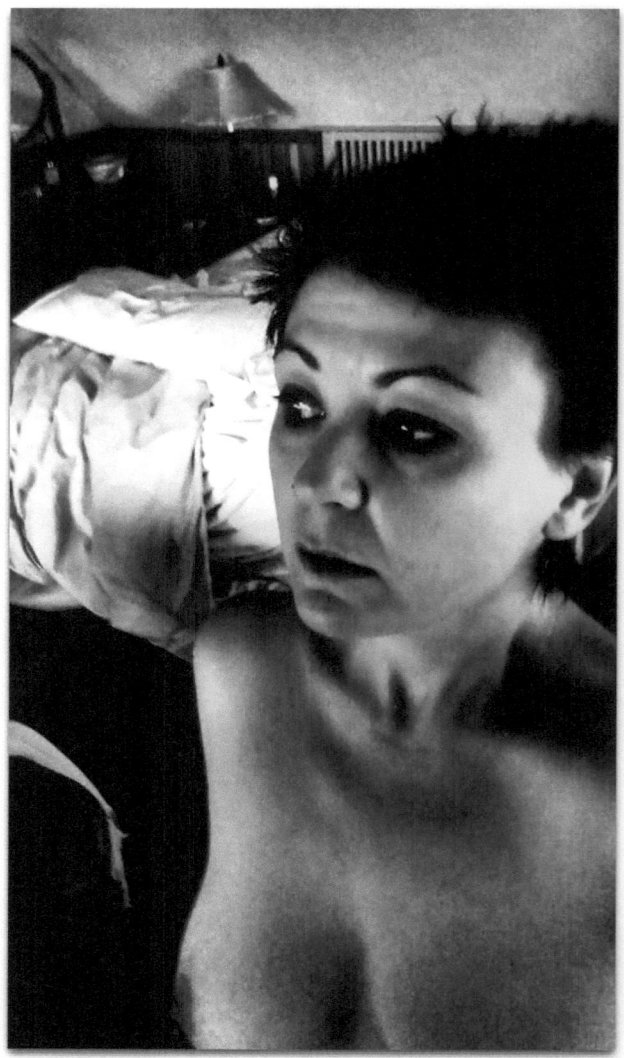

Having My Back
self portrait

Looking for More
self portrait

I'm never naked I am always wearing my tattoo. My tattoo is a collaborative piece between me and the tattoo artists I have worked with since 1998, including: Bob Tyrrell, Jennifur Cochran, and Mike Pritchett.

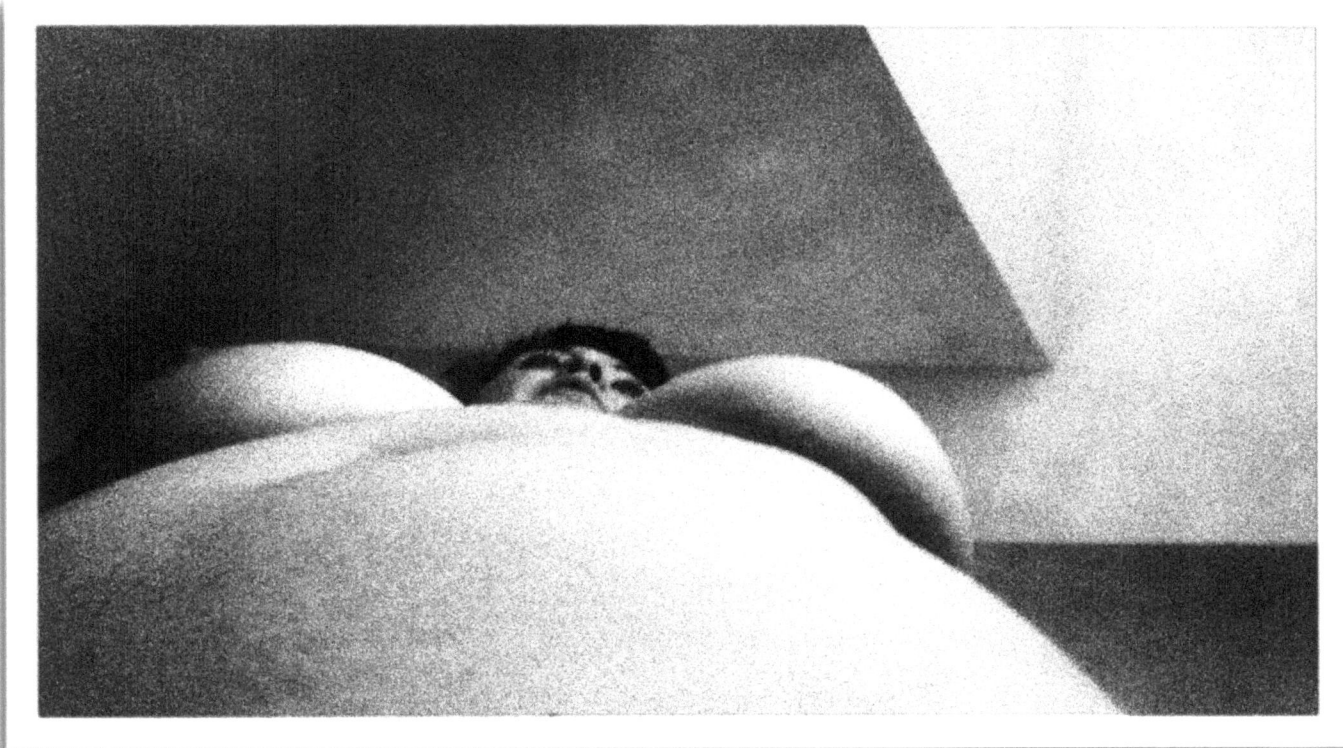

Personal Landscape
self portrait

View Out the Window
grounds at Elk Cove Inn & Spa, Elk, California

Beloved Kisses
portrait of the couple

Left: New Guinea Impatience seed pods pop at the touch of my manicured hand. Manicure by Ocean Nails, Alameda, California.

Above: United Memory portrait of the couple

Top Left: Yesterday, Today, & Tomorrow
grounds at Ekl Cove Inn & Spa, Elk, California

Bottom Left: Beach Bum Shorts
one of a kind garment customized from Decades of Style pattern 4004
shorts materials: retro card print cotton blend purchased at a garage sale, cotton quilt binding, zipper, thread
ensemble: retro bikini top from online vendor, espadrilles by Sole Society, vintage (1980's) sunglasses, second hand silk blend scarf

Right: Beach Bum View

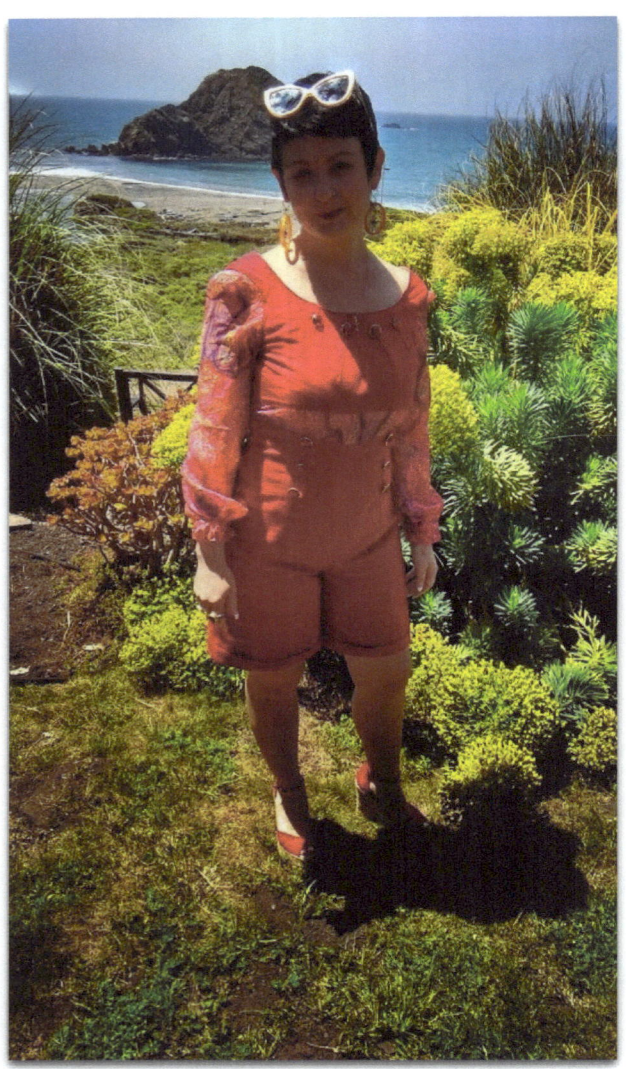 

Window Dressing
one of a kind garment
customized from burda pattern 7798 &
Decades of Style pattern 4004
dress materials: vintage (1980's) polyester
blend curtain and curtain sheer, vintage
buttons, and vintage silk ribbon purchased at
a garage sale, zipper, thread
ensemble: vintage (1980's)sun glasses,
espadrilles by Sole Society, limited edition
romantic carnelian, amethyst, grossular
garnet & sterling silver earrings (2009 Larissa
Louise)

Evening Jumper & Trousers
one of a kind garment
trousers customized from Decades of Style pattern 4004
jumper/apron original pattern by Larissa Louise
jumper materials: sustainably dyed silk/cotton blend, antique, repurposed gold pattern trim, thread
trousers materials: velvet remnants purchased at scrap depot, French cotton lace purchased at a garage sale, zipper, thread
ensemble: black tube top and jelly sandals from online vendor, my grandmother's pearls

Libations
one of a kind ensemble
trousers customized from Decades of Style
pattern 4004
trousers materials: velvet remnants
purchased at scrap depot, French cotton
lace purchased at a garage sale, zipper,
thread
ensemble: vintage (1980's) chain belt, black
tube top and jelly sandals from online
vendor
Anniversary - One of a kind custom
necklace & earring set (2013 Larissa
Louise):
sterling silver, fluorite, onyx, amethyst, white
gold diamond wedding ring, Miraculous
Medal, St. Franicis Medal

Modern/Modular Evening
(front cover also)
one of a kind ensemble
dress customized from burda pattern
7798, trousers customized from Decades
of Style pattern 4004
dress materials: organza and vintage
cotton French lace purchased at a garage
sale, antique, repurposed gold pattern
trim, vintage buttons, zipper, thread

trousers materials: velvet remnants
purchased at scrap depot, French cotton
lace purchased at a garage sale, zipper,
thread
ensemble: vintage (1980's) hand dyed silk
scarf, pointed toe flats by Sole Society

Immediate right & above: Love Clouds 1&2

Page right: Ocean Treasures 1&2

Mendocino Coast, Elk, California

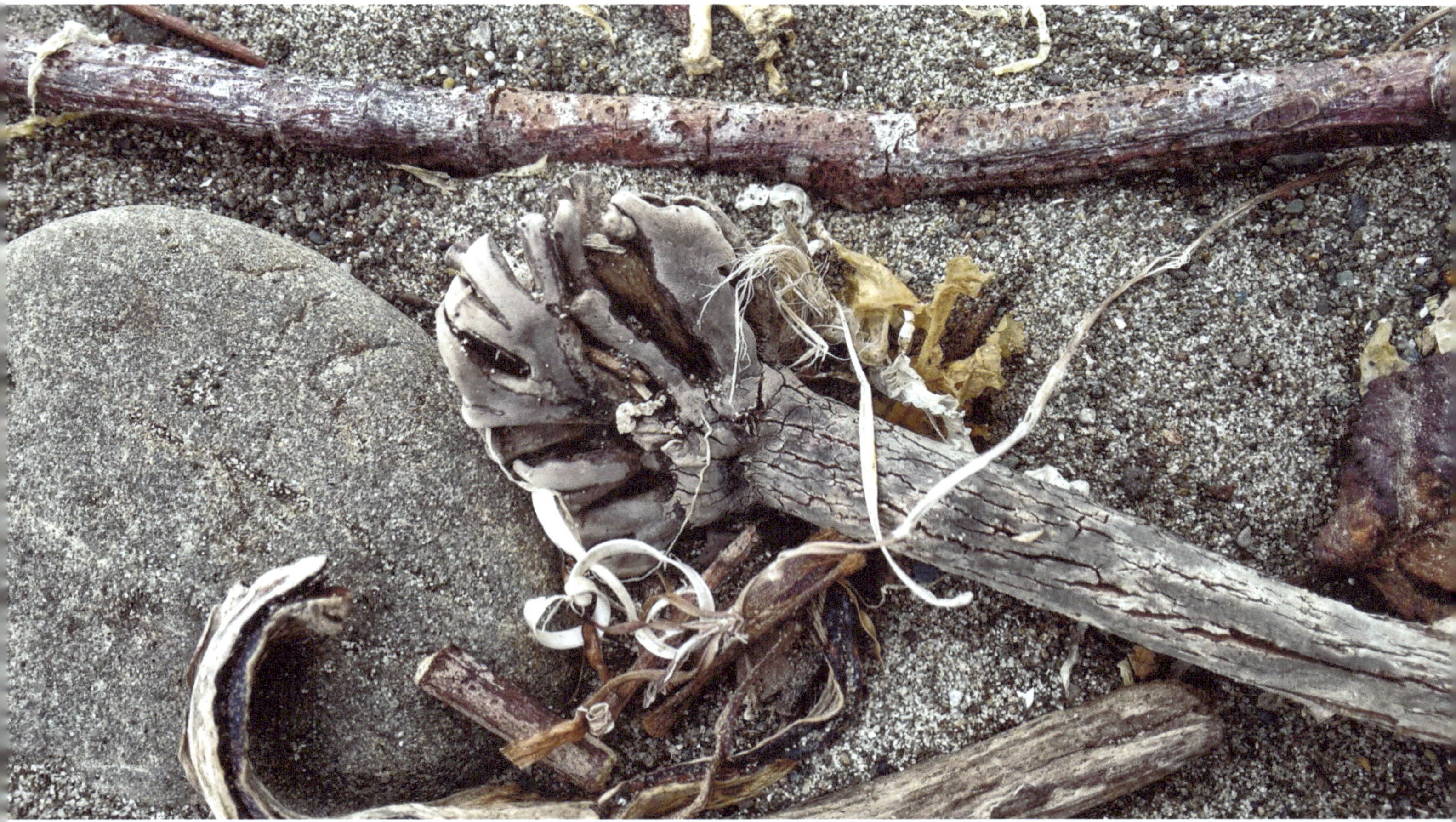

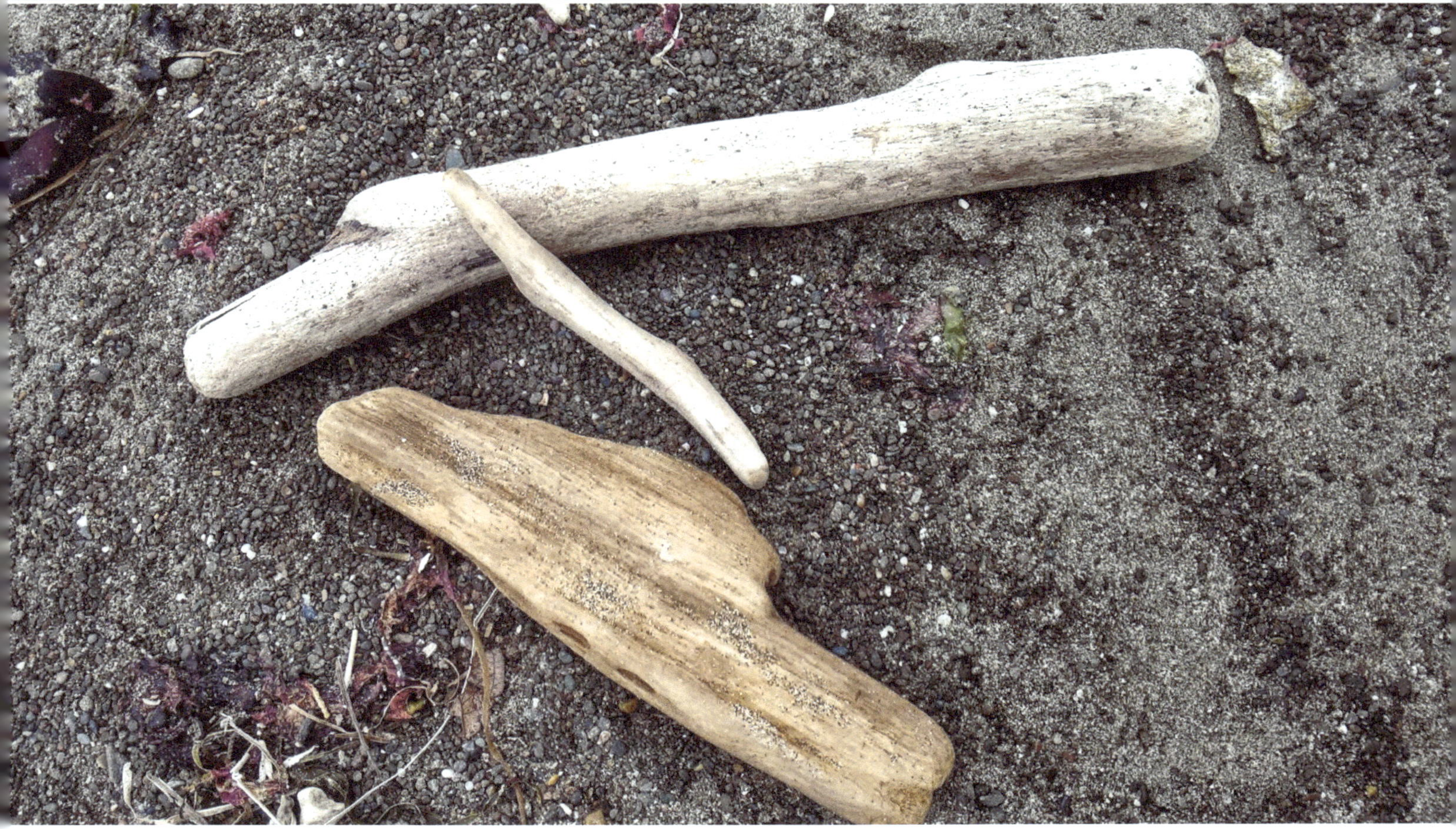

Happy Cloud Dress
one of a kind garment
dress customized from McCalls pattern
M6113
dress materials: cloud print silk
charmeuse remnants purchased at a
garage sale and sewn into yardage,
vintage button, elastic, thread

ensemble: vintage (1970's) full length half
slip, vintage (1980's) sunglasses, second
hand silk blend scarf, my grandmother's
pearls

Left: Modern/ Modular Dress
one of a kind ensemble
dress customized from burda pattern 7798
dress materials: organza and vintage cotton French lace purchased at a garage
sale, antique, repurposed gold pattern trim, vintage buttons, zipper, thread
ensemble: pointed toe flats by Sole Society, vintage pearl earrings

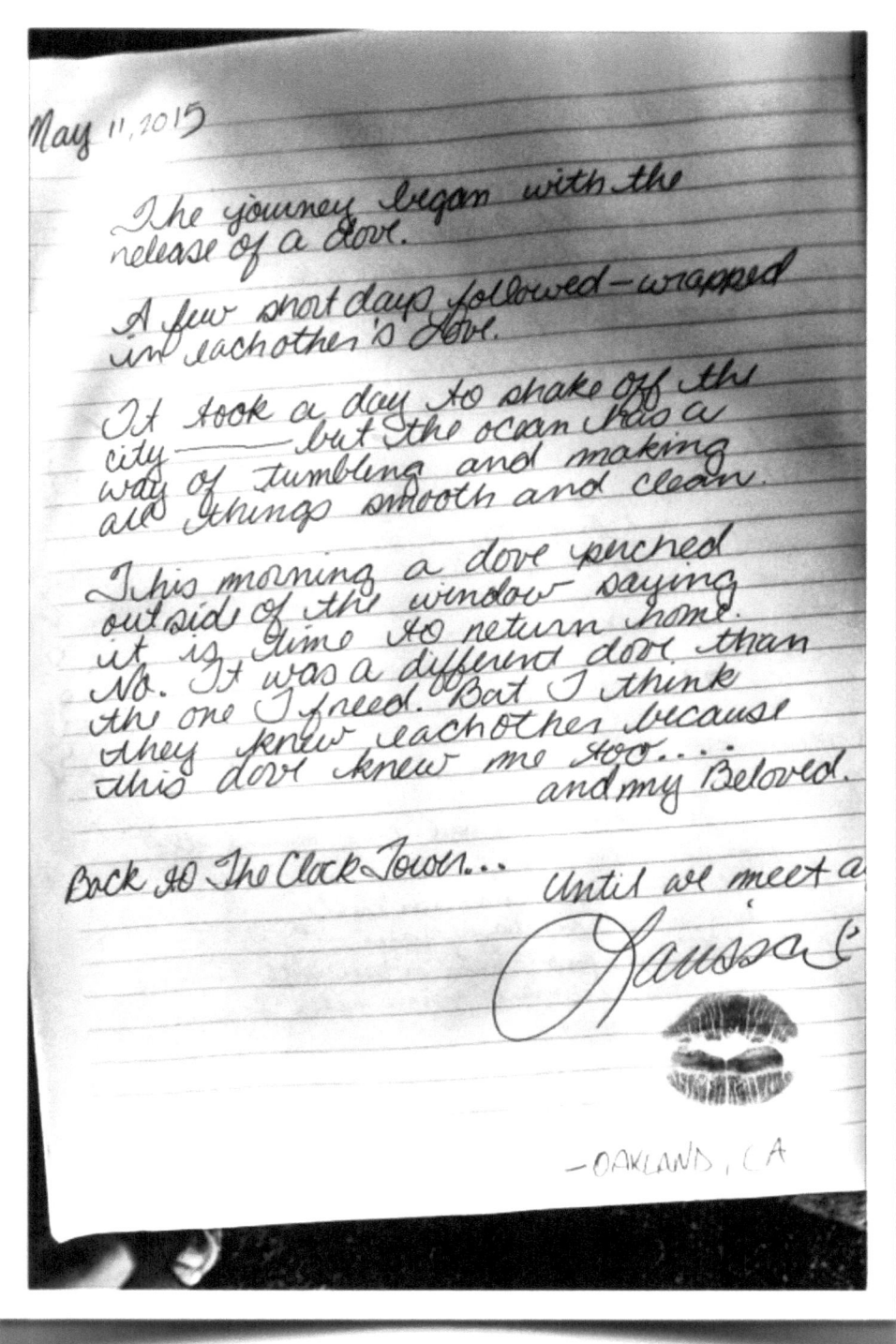

May 11, 2015

The journey began with the release of a dove.

A few short days followed — wrapped in eachother's Love.

It took a day to shake off the city ——— but the ocean has a way of tumbling and making all things smooth and clean.

This morning a dove perched outside of the window saying it is time to return home. No. It was a different dove than the one I freed. But I think they knew eachother because this dove knew me too... and my Beloved.

Back to The Clock Tower... Until we meet a

Laussa

—OAKLAND, CA